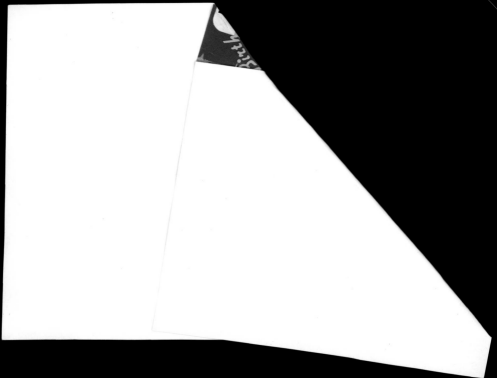

The Birthday Book

Ariel Books

Andrews and McMeel
Kansas City

10 9 8 7 6

ISBN: 0-8362-3012-4

Library of Congress Catalog Card Number:
91-77097

Design: Tilman Reitzle and Michael Hortens

The Birthday Book

*How old would you be if you didn't
know how old you are?*

—SATCHEL PAIGE

BIRTHDAYS—a time to celebrate,
a time to reflect, a time to lie about
your age! You won't be the first! The
sort-of-young and the not-so-old will
find gems in this little collection of
quotes to prompt a sly smile of recog-
nition, or raise an eyebrow, as new
light is shed on the aging issue.

Fun from start to finish, this
book is sure to add life to anyone's
years and to reiterate a resounding
"HAPPY BIRTHDAY!"

The great thing about getting older is that you don't lose all of the other ages you've been.

—MADELINE L'ENGLE

I refuse to admit that I'm more than fifty-two even if that does make my sons illegitimate.

—LADY ASTOR

Accordingly we conclude
that the appropriate age
for marriage is about the
eighteenth year for girls
and for men the thirty-
seventh plus or minus.

—ARISTOTLE

You don't stop laughing
because you grow old;
you grow old because
you stop laughing.

—MICHAEL PRITCHARD

My grandmother started walking five miles a day when she was sixty. She's ninety-seven now, and we don't know where the hell she is.

—ELLEN DEGENERIS

When I was young, the
Dead Sea was still alive.

—GEORGE BURNS

My parents didn't want
to move to Florida, but
they turned sixty, and it
was the law.

—JERRY SEINFELD

The hardest years in life
are those between ten
and seventy.

—HELEN HAYES
(AT EIGHTY-THREE)

You have to be an
antique to appreciate
them.

—FAYE MADIGAN LANGE

I am not young enough
to know everything.

—OSCAR WILDE

I smoke cigars because at my age if I don't have something to hold on to I might fall down.

—GEORGE BURNS

People who say you're
just as old as you feel
are wrong, fortunately.

—RUSSELL BAKER

Ah, but I was so much
older then
I'm younger than that
now.

—BOB DYLAN

Life is just one damned
thing after another.

—MARK TWAIN

Life is not one damned thing after another—it's the same damned thing over and over.

—EDNA ST. VINCENT MILLAY

Resolve to be tender with the young, compassionate with the aged, sympathetic with the striving, and tolerant with the weak and the wrong. Sometime in life you will have been all of these.

—BOB GODDARD

The secret of life is
enjoying the passage
of time.

—JAMES TAYLOR

Middle age is when your age starts to show around your middle.

—BOB HOPE

The blush that flies at
seventeen
Is fixed at forty-nine.

—RUDYARD KIPLING

It is not that age brings
childhood back again,
Age merely shows us
what children we remain.

—GOETHE

The denunciation of the young is a necessary part of the hygiene of older people and greatly assists in the circulation of the blood.

—LOGAN PEARSALL SMITH

I've always been told to
respect my elders and
now I've reached the age
when I don't have
anybody to respect.

—GEORGE BURNS

The true test of maturity
is not how old a person is
but how he reacts to
awakening in the midtown
area in his shorts.

—WOODY ALLEN

Middle age: when you're
sitting at home on a
Saturday night and the
phone rings and you
hope it isn't for you.

—OGDEN NASH

Zsa Zsa Gabor, when asked which of the Gabor women was the oldest, said: "She'll never admit it but I believe it's Mama."

One trouble with
growing older is that it
gets progressively harder
to find a famous
historical figure who
didn't amount to much
when he was your age.

—BILL VAUGHAN

Old age is not so bad
when you consider the
alternatives.

—MAURICE CHEVALIER

From birth to age eighteen, a girl needs parents. From age eighteen to thirty-five, she needs good looks. From thirty-five to fifty-five, a woman needs personality. And from fifty-five on, the old lady needs cash.

—KATHLEEN NORRIS

Old age is no place for
sissies.

—BETTE DAVIS

The years that a woman
subtracts from her age
are not lost. They are
added to the ages of
other women.

—DIANE DE POITIERS

Youth is a disease from
which we all recover.

—DOROTHY FULDHEIM

If you survive long
enough, you're revered—
rather like an old
building.

—KATHARINE HEPBURN

The old believe
everything, the middle-
aged suspect everything,
the young know
everything.

—OSCAR WILDE

Live as long as you may,
the first twenty years are
the longest half of your
life.

—ROBERT SOUTHEY

I am constantly amazed when I talk to young people to learn how much they know about sex and how little about soap.

—BILLIE BURKE

When I was a boy of fourteen, my father was so ignorant I could hardly stand to have the old man around. But when I got to be twenty-one, I was astonished at how much the old man had learned in seven years.

—MARK TWAIN

As far as I remember,
twenty-one was a devilish
age. . .

—VIRGINIA WOOLF

For a young man, a
woman of thirty has
irresistible attractions.

—HONORÉ DE BALZAC

Grow up, and that is a
terribly hard thing to do.
It is much easier to skip
it and go from one
childhood to another.

—F. Scott Fitzgerald

It is better to waste one's
youth than to do nothing
with it at all.

—GEORGE COURTELINE

A majority of young
people seem to develop
mental arteriosclerosis
forty years before they
get the physical kind.

—ALDOUS HUXLEY

Young men think old
men are fools; but old
men know young men
are fools.

—GEORGE CHAPMAN

At twenty years of age,
the will reigns; at thirty,
the wit; and at forty, the
judgment.

—BENJAMIN FRANKLIN

The secret of staying young is to live honestly, eat slowly, and lie about your age.

—LUCILLE BALL

I have everything now I
had twenty years ago—
except now it's all lower.

—GYPSY ROSE LEE

The lovely thing about
being forty is that you
can appreciate twenty-
five-year-old men more.

—COLLEEN MCCULLOUGH

Youth is the gift of
nature, but age is a work
of art.

—GARSON KANIN

Never trust a woman
who wears mauve,
whatever her age may be,
or a woman over thirty-
five who is fond of pink
ribbons. It always means
that they have a history.

—OSCAR WILDE

The first forty years of life furnish the text, while the remaining thirty supply the commentary.

—ARTHUR SCHOPENHAUER

We don't understand life
any better at forty than
at twenty, but we know it
and admit it.

—JULES RENARD

The man who is not a
socialist at twenty has no
heart, but if he is still a
socialist at forty he has
no head.

—ARISTIDE BRIAND

Every man over forty is a scoundrel.

—BERNARD SHAW

Years ago we discovered the exact point, the dead center of middle age. It occurs when you are too young to take up golf and too old to rush up to the net.

—FRANKLIN P. ADAMS

One of the chief
pleasures of middle age is
looking back at all the
people you didn't marry.

—ANONYMOUS

You know you're getting
older when the candles
cost more than the cake.

—BOB HOPE

The years between fifty
and seventy are the
hardest. You are always
being asked to do things,
and yet you are not
decrepit enough to turn
them down.

—T. S. ELIOT

Everything got better
after I was fifty.

—A. J. P. TAYLOR

I'm fifty-three years old
and six feet four. I've had
three wives, five children
and three grandchildren.
I love good whiskey. I
still don't understand
women, and I don't think
there is any man who
does.

—JOHN WAYNE

The lunches of fifty-seven
years had caused his
chest to slip down to the
mezzanine floor.

—P. G. WODEHOUSE